COSMIC DOODLINGS

FOR SELF-REALIZATION

AND SELF-COLORING

by Elan Z. Neev

△geless Books #3

II

To my earthly and cosmic parents, with love

I guess you did create me for a reason!
Thank you...

III

COSMIC DOODLINGS IS
A HAPPY BOOK BY A HAPPY
SOUL FOR HAPPY SOULS
(OR THOSE SEEKING TO BE
HAPPY), FOR HAPPINESS'
SAKE (ALSO FOR GOD'S
SAKE!) AND FOR LIGHT.

To be happy despite the suffering that afflicts you is to bring salvation to the world.

The Divine Spirit doesn't reside but in the joyful heart

Thoughts from the Talmud

CONTENTS

HOW TO USE THIS BOOK

The answer is: Well! In my book
WHOLISTIC HEALING: HOW TO HARMONIZE
YOUR BODY, MIND AND SPIRIT WITH
LIFE — for freedom, joy, health,
beauty, love, money and psychic
powers, I said on page 92, "In this
Aquarian Age, many of us are, indeed, in
touch with the process of rejuvenation.
The prerequisite to experiencing reju—
venation, or at least retarding aging,
is to keep the natural child within
our souls playing freely, happily
and creatively. Some humor, some
mischievousness, some blind trust, some
unconditional Eros, some fantasy — will
go a long way to promoting Wholistic
health and joyous longevity."

On page 5 of WHOLISTIC HEALING I said,
"The next step, after we stop insisting
on a logical, intellectual explanation—
or any explanation at all — is to allow
our fancy to flow free."

Carry this Cosmic Doodlings book with
you wherever you go, to bring the
light to every situation and to share
it with others. This light may bring
a smile to your face, or may dry a tear,

or you may iron out a wrinkle, as it spreads relaxation and peace of mind and soul. When you are relaxed and disarmed, the seeds of divine truth and cosmic consciousness may penetrate via this light to take root and blossom with the celestial rhythm of life - from within your mind and heart and every cell, atom, sub-atom, sub-sub-atom... and from within every process known or unknown to you or to science...

This is your personal copy. It exchanges energy with you. Color it for fun, and exchange even more energy as you meditate through art and color. Show it to your friends, but don't give or lend your personal copy. Instead, buy new copies to give as gifts of love and joy. If you are a teacher, have your students "study" it and meditate over it to get in touch with some profound and abstract truths that can be focused on and applied for fuller and better living.

The more individuals apply this book, the more people will travel light the path of life and the more light will shine: through us onto our universe, and back upon us from this wonderful creation...

CHAPTER

The World or
It's not nice to cheat mother nature

3

4

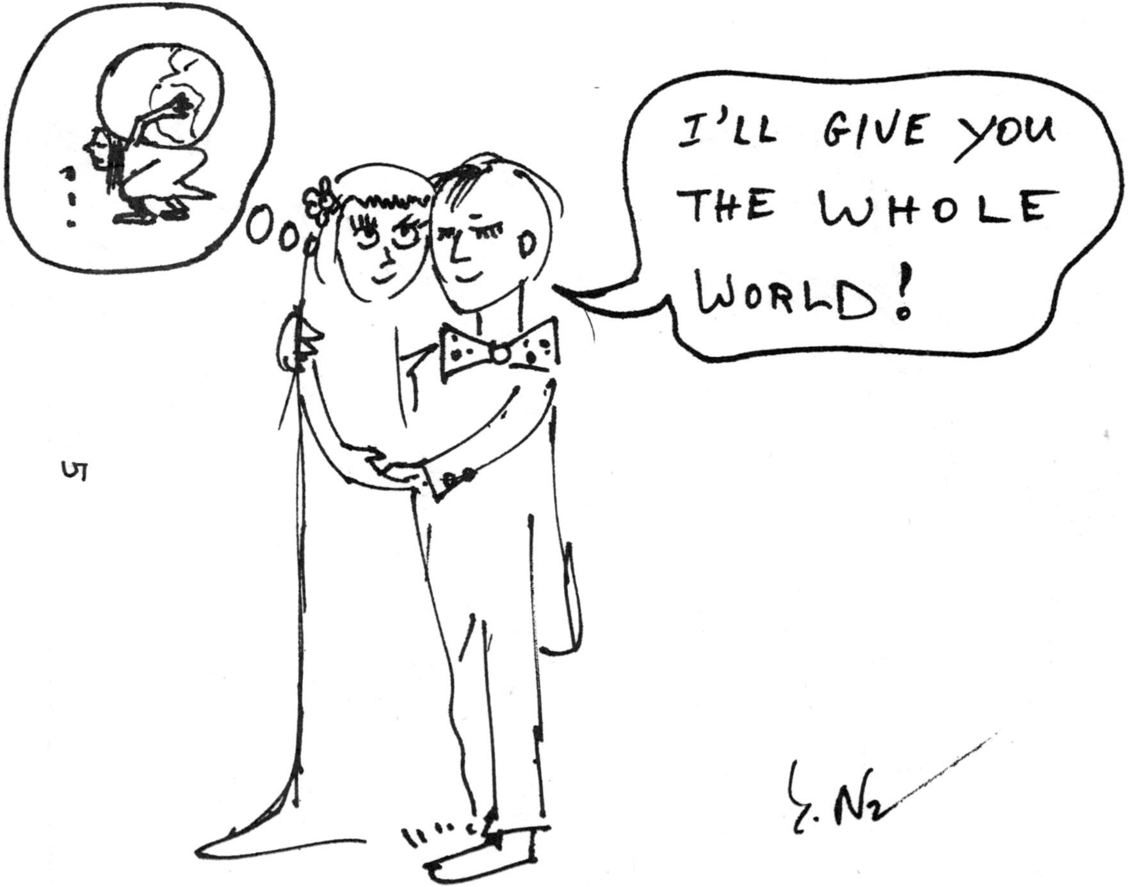
I'LL GIVE YOU THE WHOLE WORLD!

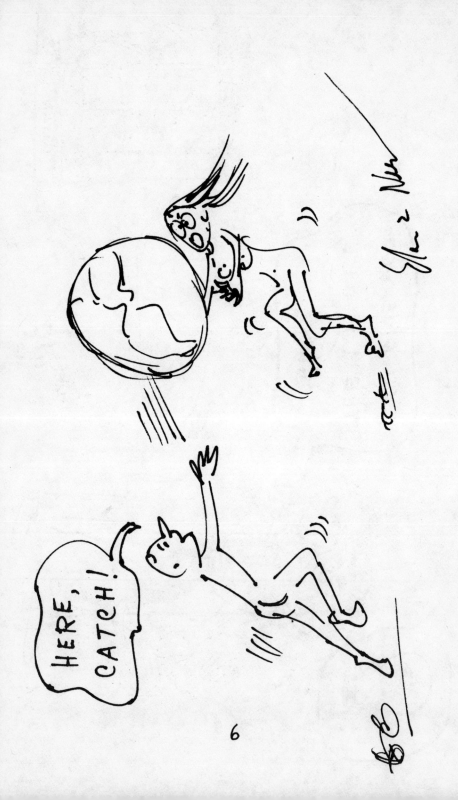

6

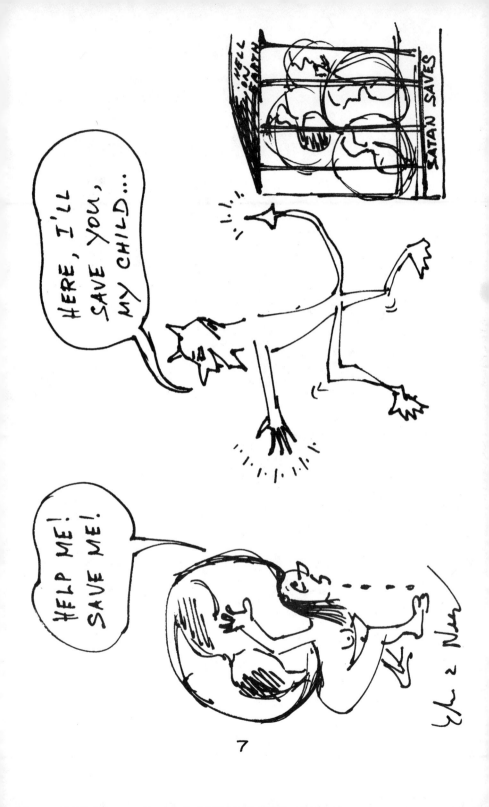

7

9

10

CHAPTER

(me!)

14

15

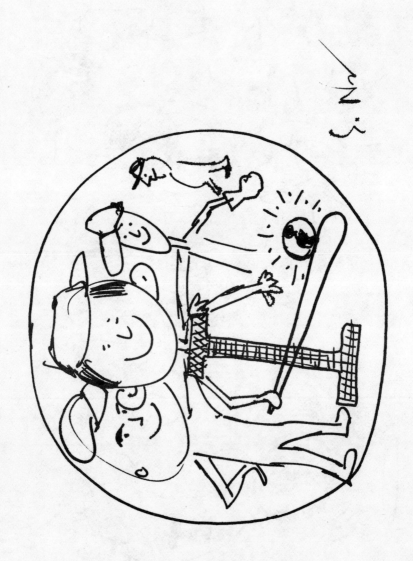

CHAPTER

turn OVER

COSMIC AIKIDO

AIKIDO is the Japanese art of self-defense in harmony with the *KI* — the life force. At *SII* we expand and 'WHOLICIZE' aikido to deal with all aspects of our lives — not only self-defense. We teach how to turn <u>all</u> experiences, painful ones included, and all forces — including opposing forces — to work for us and for the highest good.

20

The secret of Aikido is to harmonize ourselves with the natural movement of the Universe, to bring ourselves into accord with the Universe Itself. One who has realized the secret of Aikido has the Universe within, and can say "I am the Universe."

O'Sensei Morihei Ueshiba
Founder of Aikido

FROM ISOMETRIC
DEVELOPMENT
TO COSMIC AIKIDO...

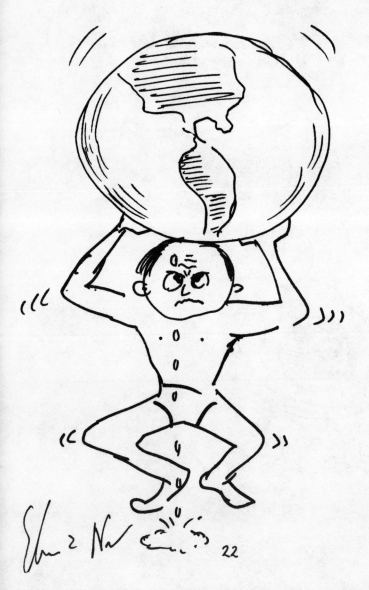

22

25

CHAPTER

Growth

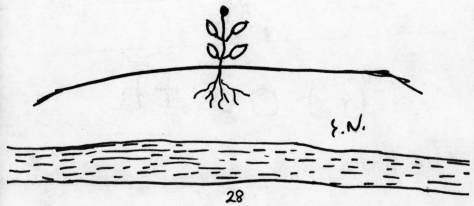

E.N.

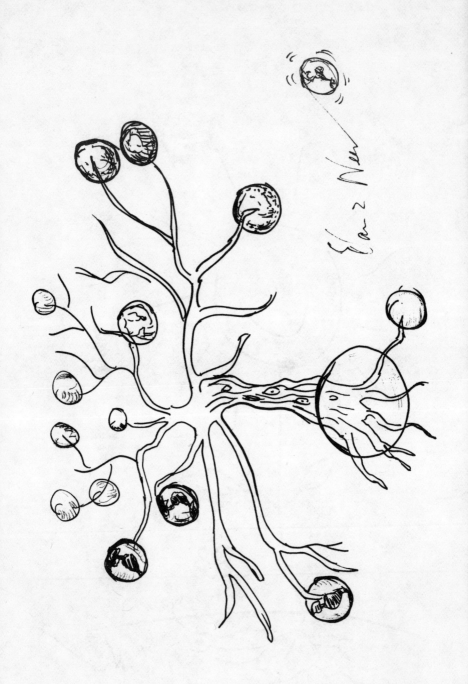

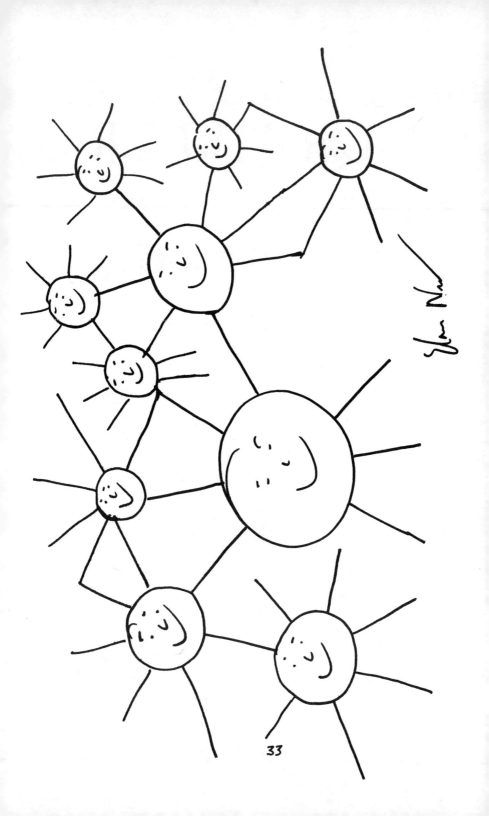

CHAPTER

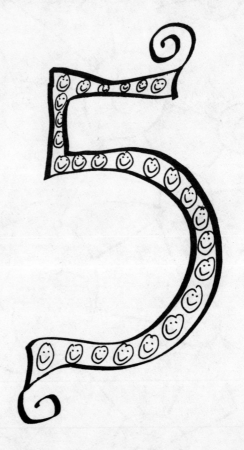

Awareness

LOW CONSCIOUSNESS

PAST

FUTURE

35

HIGH CONSCIOUSNESS
EXPANDED AWARENESS

"PAST"

LOW CONSCIOUSNESS
LIMITED AWARENESS

"FUTURE"

36

37

TRUTH ?!

(FROM DR. NEEV'S WHOLISTIC HEALING: HOW TO HARMONIZE YOUR BODY, MIND AND SPIRIT WITH LIFE. Published by AGELESS BOOKS.)

41

A PORTRAIT OF
A RICH PERSON

WITHIN...WITHIN...WORLDS WITHIN WORLDS... WITHIN WORLDS... WITHIN WORLDS... WITHIN WORLDS... WITHIN WORLDS

45

CHAPTER

Relationships

NEUROTIC RELATIONSHIP
(ALL IN THE FAMILY)

BAD RELATIONSHIP - ENTANGLEMENT

GOOD RELATIONSHIP — SPACIOUS....

KARMIC RELATIONSHIP

NO FIRE!!

BUT I AM COLD!

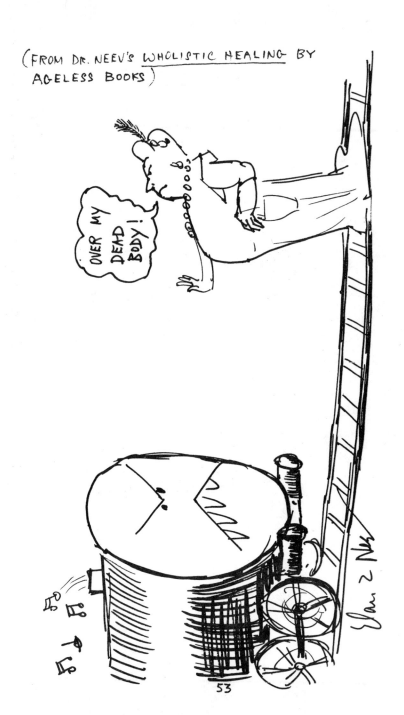

MIRROR, MIRROR ON THE WALL
I DO LOVE MY NEIGHBORS AS ME... ALL!

(FROM DR. NEEV'S <u>WHOLISTIC HEALING</u>
BY AGELESS BOOKS)

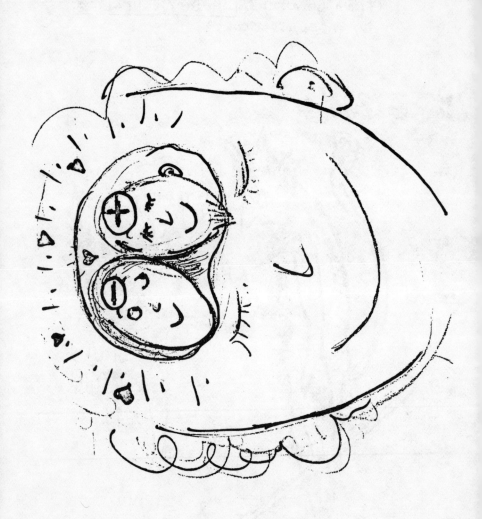

DIVINITY FOUND, EXPRESSED AND FULFILLED

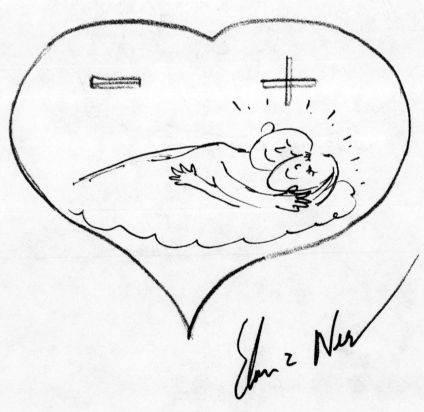

If you do not find worthwhile benefits for others, exapnd your goal to include them, for your own good. BY INCLUDING OTHERS, YOU INTENSIFY THE ENERGIES PULLING AND PUSHING TOWARD THE REALIZATION OF YOUR GOAL.

Even if your goal includes the good of others, make sure the fact is paramount in your awareness and that in meditation you perceive all those "others" sharing in the joys of your success.

FOR MY OWN GOAL EXPANSION, I ENVISION THIS BOOK HELPING PEOPLE ALL OVER THE WORLD. THIS WILL BRING ME GREAT SPIRITUAL AND FINANCIAL REWARD, MUCH OF WHICH I WISH TO RETURN IN THE FORM OF CREATING AN INTERNATIONAL SCHOOL OF COMMUNICATIONS FOR UNIVERSAL CONSCIOUSNESS AT THE UNITED NATIONS. IN THIS WAY, I HOPE TO EXPAND THE CONSCIOUSNESS OF WORLD LEADERS, THEREBY FURTHERING UNIVERSAL HARMONY THROUGH WORLD PEACE, PROSPERITY AND EVOLUTION.

(A PAGE FROM DR. NEEV'S WHOLISTIC HEALING BY AGELESS BOOKS) 60

CHAPTER

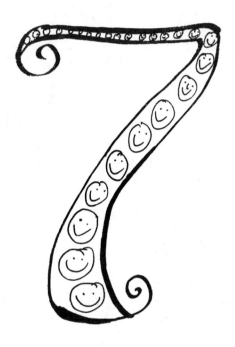

7

Light Touch of Light from around The World

Do not cut you own roots, even
if your roots are in deep manure.
Instead turn the manure into
fertilization to nourish your beautiful
tree of life, to bear fruit, and
to touch branches with other trees.

American Indian

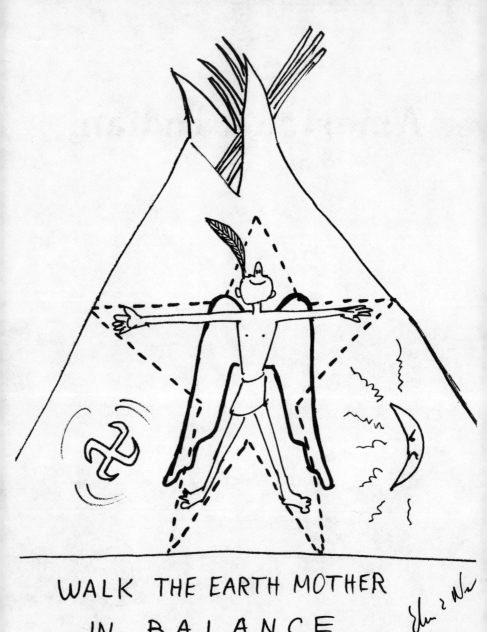

WALK THE EARTH MOTHER
IN BALANCE

AMERICAN INDIAN PRECEPT

64

Buddhism

This world is a mansion of mirth; here I can eat, drink and celebrate

RAMAKRISHNA

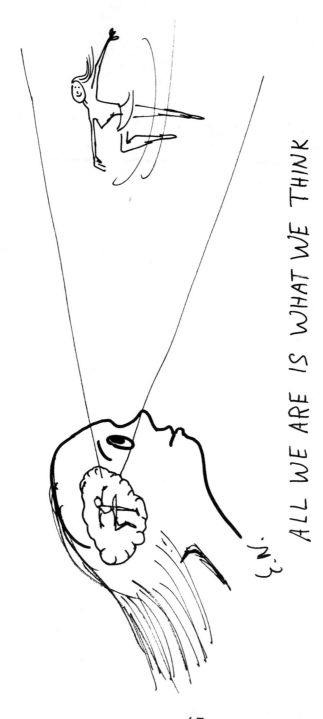

ALL WE ARE IS WHAT WE THINK

DAMMAPADA

67

Christianity

69

Confucianism

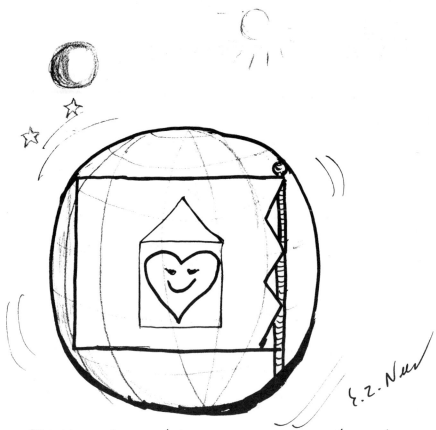

If there is righteousness in the heart,
there will be beauty in the character.

If there is beauty in the character,
there will be harmony in the home.

If there is harmony in the home,
there will be order in the nation.

If there is order in the nation,
there will be peace in the world.

The Great Learning

Hermetism

THE
ALL

THE UNIVERSE IS MENTAL —
HELD IN THE MIND OF
THE ALL...
The Kybalion

½ the truth

The other half

AS ABOVE
SO BELOW.

The Kybalion

EVERYTHING IS DUAL... EXTREMES
MEET; ALL TRUTHS ARE BUT HALF-TRUTHS;
ALL PARADOXES MAY BE RECONCILED.

The Kybalion

Knowledge, like wealth,
Is intended for use.

The Kybalion

Hinduism

JNANA YOGA — the path of knowledge

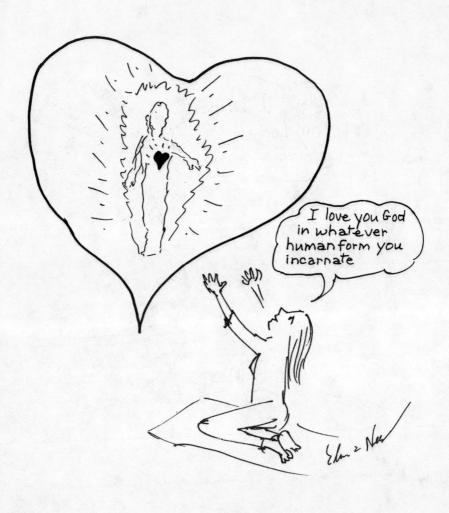

BHAKTI YOGA – the path of love

KARMA YOGA – the path of work

Doctor Swami Sigmunanda Freud's
Layered cake (yammi!!)
an old recipe for the hungry soul

The Wheel of Life and the angles on the Truth

Give up all varieties of religion and just surrender to Me. I will guard you from all sinful reactions.

Bhagavad-Gita

Huna

HUNA = SECRET

- ## MANA = LIFE FORCE.
- ## ANO = SEED. ○ HOU = RESTORE, breathe heavily.
- ## HO = MAKE.

- Superconscious
- Conscious
- subconscious

The seed of secret is left... for you to investigate!

HO-ANO = to worship (to make a seed, to plant)
ANO-HOU = the answer for a prayer (restore the seed by breathing in Mana, life force).

Islam

Let there be no compulsion in religion...
The Koran

WILL YOU THEN FORCE MEN TO BELIEVE WHEN BELIEF CAN COME FROM GOD ONLY?!
Muhammed

Judaism

HEAR, O ISRAEL, THE LORD THE LORD OUR GOD, IS ONE

Thou shalt love the the Lord, thy God with all thy heart, with all thy soul, and with all thy might.
Old Testament

89

92

If I am not for myself, who will be?
And being for my own self only, what am I?
And if not now, when?

      Rabbi Hillel in Pirke Avot.

Mayan

Life is a
flower which
is offered to the Gods....
   Based on Mayan thoughts........

Taoism

Those who flow as life,
know
they need no other force

The Tao Te Ching
97

Zoroastrianism

OBJECT:
Truth.
That alone
can make
man Godlike,
whose body is
like light and
whose soul
like truth.

Zoroastrian precept.

CHAPTER

Cosmic Doodlings About Us

COSMIC DOODLINGS ABOUT US
(Sii or Self-Improvement Institute)

Why here and now?

An ancient Hebrew sage said in Pirke Avot, "He whose wisdom is greater than his deeds, what is he like? Like a tree whose branches are many and whose roots are a few; and the wind comes and uproots it and overturns it on its face."

We believe in translating the cosmic and divine knowledge into our everyday life. Writing and publishing is one way we acomplish our mission of light. Giving lectures, private consultations and intensive workshops, is another.

Through personal interaction we help you integrate this knowledge on a very deep level so it blossoms from within you and your world. Then you put those

101

beautiful ideas to practice.

what do we do?

We help you heal or prevent
the New Age disease
we diagnose as

<u>spiritual</u>

<u>indigestion</u>. This is a painful
disease of knowing <u>what</u> to do
but not <u>how</u> to do it; of having
unintegrated information, some-
times conflicting.

WE TRAIN PEOPLE TO EXPERIENCE ONENESS

We help people remove blocks to the
life energy flow and to the awareness
of oneness and
wholeness on
all levels...

Anger
fear
guilt
compulsion
addiction
toxin
prejudice

102

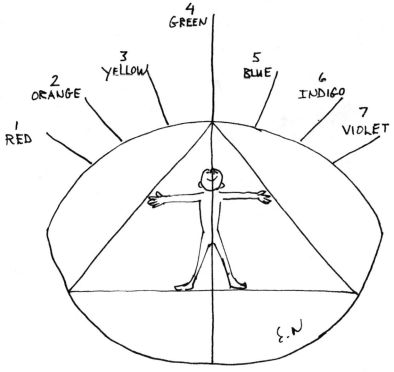

We help people link to the Infinite
and experience limitless abundance
in all that is good...

We synergize the best of most
paths to create a powerful
wholistic approach to
creative, free, joyous living—
to fulfill individual and
group missions.

We transcend together the
differences and barriers,
and become self-realized.

I AM DIVINE

אֲנִי

יהוה

WE HELP PEOPLE
EXPERIENCE GOD
REGARDLESS OF
AGE, FAITH AND
SPIRITUAL
EVOLUTION.
(There is no time left!)

If I Were a Gardener

If I were a gardener I would want to have humanity as a garden of flowers of all colors, kinds, creeds, fragrances. I wouldn't force them to cross and become alike, because I love multiplicity of color, form, vibration.... But I would allow those who wish, to cross, and I would enjoy the new hues and breeds and beauty. I would treat them all with loving kindness according to their own needs, individuality, specialness... and as a garden.

E.Z.N.

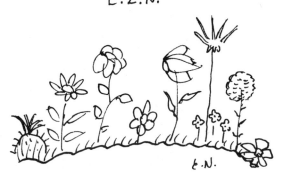

E.N.

The law is living word of living God to living prophets for living men. In everything that is life is the law written. You find it in the grass, in the tree, in the river, in the mountain, in the birds of heaven, in the fishes of the sea; but seek it chiefly in yourselves.

Quoted by permission from the Essene Gospel of Peace, book one, page 13, translated from the third century Aramaic manuscript by Edmond Bordeaux Szekely, published by Biogenic Society International, apartado 372, Cartago, Costa Rica, Central America.

An afterthought, from the Talmud

Judge your fellow always with a leaning to the side of merit.

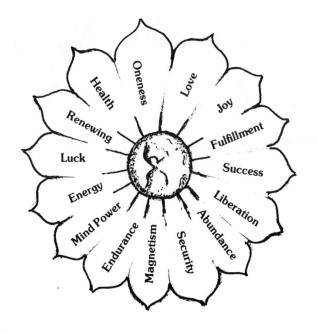

Health Oneness Love Joy Fulfillment Success Liberation Abundance Security Magnetism Endurance Mind Power Energy Luck Renewing

To inquire about our books,
tapes, lectures, workshops
and private sessions (in
person or from a distance) - or
to comment on this book — send
your letters (print your name,
please, and include your phones)
to Sii, P.O.B 6300, Beverly Hills,
Ca. 90212, or dial (213) 933-NEEV.

WHAT SHALL I DO WITH THIS INSERT?

IT'S FUN TO SHARE <u>COSMIC DOODLINGS</u> (and good for your Karma, too!). If you are with us in spirit, give this insert to a deserving soul, or buy extra copies of <u>Cosmic Doodlings</u> for your friends.(If you lend your personal copy, you may as well kiss it goodbye!) It's a great gift for Christmas, Chanuka and birthdays. <u>SUGGESTION</u>: Show this insert to your favorite book-stores to order more copies. If they are out of <u>Cosmic Doodlings</u> and you want your fun books now, you may order directly from Ageless Books, P.O. Box 6300, Beverly Hills, CA 90212, by sending $6.90 for each copy. For faster service, please enclose a re-turn address label.

If you are a 'Big Timer' and wish to widen the circle of love and joy, you may order 10 or more copies and deduct $2.00 per copy (which is appro-ximately 30%). And if you fancy being a distributor of fun and light, let us know. You may get more than a 50% discount on large quantities of <u>Cosmic Doodlings, Wholistic Healing</u>, Self-Improvement Tapes and more.

P.S.: Wholistic Healing is $5.90 for the soft cover and $11 for the deluxe hard cover.

Readers Acclaim

Through cartoons and a few words, COSMIC DOODLINGS transmits abstract truths from great thinkers and spiritual masters into a form delightfully under-stood by people of all ages and backgrounds. It entertains, inspires, and instructs. It brings the New Age home to the child within. It helps people free themselves from the limitations of their se-parateness and ushers them into the joyous aware-ness of their Oneness. As an enthusiastic graduate of Dr. Elan Z. Neev's 40-hour ONENESS TRAINING, I am happy for COSMIC DOODLINGS to see the light of the world and for the world to see the light of COSMIC DOODLINGS.

ToniLove Gabriel, Ph.D.

As a medical doctor researching rejuvenation, I was surprised to discover the wealth of information and the masterkeys to healings imparted by Dr. Elan Z. Neev in his short, easy-to-read book WHOLISTIC HEALING. I was even more amazed to see what Dr. Neev does with another short and simple book of cartoons COSMIC DOODLINGS. In this, he reviews mas-terkeys to consciousness, growth and to comparative religion and philosophy that impart a healing of the human spirit. So deep and yet so light and amusing! Indeed, this book can easily be a fascinating way to laughter and rejuvenation through art and creative intelligence.

Joy Hentrup, M.D.

Dr. Elan Z. Neev is a jack of all trades and a master of some. One of his pet goals in meditation is "maximum utilization of all ... about oneness, fulfillment, joy, love, prosperity and enlightenment to me, and through me, to all."

This book is one cosmic gift in answer to his prayer. It may be a cosmic gift in answer to your prayer, too.

Dr. Neev is the founder-director of the Self-Improvement Institute whose motto is Harmony with Life Thru Wholistic Awareness, and the author of Wholistic Healing: How to Harmonize Your Body, Mind and Spirit with Life. Enjoy!...

COSMIC DOODLINGS

FOR SELF-REALIZATION

AND SELF-COLORING

by Elan Z. Neev

Ageless Books #3

495   ISBN 0-918482-03-8